CONTENTS

THE GAMERS' HANDBOOK

STAYING SAFE ONLINE

Online gaming should be fun and interactive. You can play with friends or with people across the globe.

To keep it fun, make sure that you stay safe and know how to protect yourself and your personal information while playing online. Before you start playing, there are a few simple guidelines that you should bear in mind.

Once these are in place, you can relax, enjoy gaming and prevent any problems later.

IT'S YOUR GAME

You can't always be sure that a player is who they say they are, so use a cool game name to stay safe. Using an avatar instead of the webcam will protect your anonymity, and some games have voice alteration.

Learn how to block or report a player if they are making you uncomfortable, and tell a trusted adult what has happened.

A CLEAN MACHINE

Computer viruses, spyware and other bugs can ruin your gaming, so talk to your parents or guardians and make sure all devices that connect to the internet are protected. Installing the latest security software, web browser, and operating system will make everyone more secure.

PROTECT YOUR INFO

Personal information is anything that can be used to identify you, such as your name, address, phone number, pictures, or birthday. Make passwords strong with capital and lowercase letters, numbers and symbols. Don't share them with anyone, except your parents or guardians.

INTRO TO GAMING

A QUICK LOOK AT THE HISTORY OF VIDEO GAMES

Video games have only been around for about sixty years and they have changed an awful lot in that time. Here are some of the milestones from Pong to Fortnite.

1958

A nuclear scientist invents the first video game Tennis for Two to show off his work at an open day.

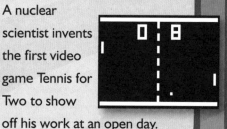

1972

Atari Pong is the first arcade game and a huge smash. It earns four times as much as other machines.

1977

The Atari 2600 brings the joystick to gaming – two actually, so you could play games against another person. The unit costs $199 and turns millions of people on to home gaming. The games were in colour and were on interchangeable cartridges so you could play different games on one console.

1978

Space Invaders arrives and brings glory to some as one of the first games to save the highest scoring player's name.

1980

Pac-Man starts munching his way around the arcades of the world. Ms Pac-Man becomes the biggest selling arcade game ever.

1981

Nintendo's Donkey Kong introduces us to Mario, or as he was known then, Jumpman. Nintendo only came up with Mario because they couldn't get a licence for a game based on Popeye. The plump Italian plumber has now appeared in more than 200 games, as well as films, TV and comics.

1984

A Russian mathematician invents Tetris, which spreads around the world to become one of the most popular games of all time.

1989

Gaming goes mobile with Nintendo's Game Boy, which uses cartridge games to play. It has sold over 120 million units.

1991

Sonic the Hedgehog arrives as the hero of Sega games, but he could have been a dog, a rabbit, an old man, or an armadillo – all ideas that were considered. Sega asked random people which they liked best before deciding. Just as well – Sonic has sold 800 million games.

1995

The first Sony Playstation is launched and became the first console to sell 100 million, just under ten years later.

1996

Action gaming heroine Lara Croft is born. Tomb Raider was created in Derby, where a road is named after her.

1997

After five years in development, Sony release driving game Gran Turismo for the Playstation. It went on to sell more than 10 million copies and is rated one of the best driving games ever. The developer said he only went home for four days a year when developing the game.

2001

Microsoft gets into gaming when the Xbox is launched and quickly becomes a leader in online gaming.

2004

Nintendo DS is the next step for handhelds with dual screen action, stylus touchscreen and cool games such as Pokémon and Spider-Man.

2005

Guitar Hero brings the coolest controller ever to the world of gaming. Would-be guitar stars are given the chance to 'strap on their axe' and play along to their favourite rock anthems. It's so popular that there are soon drum kits, microphones and DJ turntables.

2010

Minecraft brings building blocks to the online world, makes the developer a billionaire, and makes millions of players happy.

2017

Fortnite becomes one of the fastest growing games of all time with more than 200 million people registered to play.

INTRODUCING THE DIFFERENT TYPES OF GAMING GENRES

You're a gamer, but what kind of games are right for you? This may seem like a strange question, but there are actually many different types of games, so before you go out and spend money on something that you may not like, it's worth having a look at the main genres.

These pages have a breakdown of the various types of video games, what they are like to play and the skills they require. You will also find real examples of games from each section. Some games cover more than one genre so you may find certain games in more than one section.

 235 **2** **5**

MULTIPLAYER ONLINE GAMES

You'll never be short of a partner with these multiplayer games as there can be hundreds of other people online at the same time. Have you got what it takes to stand out from the crowd?

See page 32

SIMULATION GAMES

A simulator puts you in control of something that might never happen to you in real life. Whether that's flying a jet, driving a racing car, or managing a zoo or farm, it feels real and you're in charge.

See page 34

ACTION AND ADVENTURE

These games combine the excitement of action games where you need great reactions and coordination, with the problem-solving and strategy of adventure games. Players get the best of both worlds.

See page 36

STRATEGY GAMES

You have to concentrate for a long time when it comes to strategy games. Players have to make choices during the game that will affect what happens to their character as the game progresses.

See page 38

EDUCATIONAL GAMES

Learning doesn't have to be boring with the help of educational gaming. There are lots of titles that will help with schoolwork such as maths, history, vocabulary and science. Even your parents will be happy that you're gaming. *See page 40*

COMBAT GAMES

Classic combat games let players pit their skills and best moves against each other. Whether it's through shoot-outs, sword fights, martial arts, or boxing, there is a combat choice for you. Choose your weapons carefully.

See page 42

SPORT GAMES

Everyone loves sport, and games let the fun continue even when you are stuck indoors or are short of players for your team. From football to snowboarding, sports titles are now so realistic that e-sports could end up in the Olympic Games.

See page 44

DRIVING GAMES

You may not be old enough to take your driving test, but driving games allow you to hit the highway and feel the need for speed. Choose your vehicle, customise it, and put your pedal to the metal and try to stay on the track.

See page 46

FANTASY GAMES

There's nothing like going on an adventure to a place that is beyond your dreams. With fantasy games, you can escape to amazing worlds to meet strange characters and exotic creatures, creating your own fantastic journey.

See page 48

ACTIVITY GAMES

Not all games are about sitting in front of a screen. A growing number of games make you jump up, jump about, play an instrument, sing, or dance. And it's a fun way to burn off some of your energy and have lots of fun along the way.

See page 50

ENSURE MAXIMUM COMFORT LEVELS

If you love to play games then you will be spending
a lot of time doing it, so it makes sense to take a little
bit of time beforehand to make sure that your gaming
set up is perfect for you. Follow these pointers to
make sure that you are in the zone to game.
Then sit back, relax and prepare to have fun.

HEADSETS

An over-ear headset can make you feel like you are part of the action. Check sound levels before gaming – you don't want to damage your ears. Pick headphones with a mic if you need to chat.

SCREENS

Make sure that your monitor is in a place where you see the action without straining your eyes or getting a neck ache. Block out any glare from sunlight coming in through windows, and give the screen a wipe with a microfibre cloth before playing.

CONTROLLERS

Untangle the cables before you get started and make sure that controllers are fully charged, or that you have spare batteries on standby.

SEATING

You can get special gaming seats with built-in speakers and even motion simulation, but the main thing is to be comfortable. Choose a seat that you like to sit in and test some positions. Do you need a footrest or some cushions to make it perfect? **You are now ready to play!**

LET'S GET GAMING

WHAT VIDEO GAME SHOULD I PLAY?

You're ready to play, but what's the game for you? There are hundreds that you could try, so take our quick and fun quiz to help you decide what game genres you'll enjoy most.

1. WHAT DO YOU MOST WANT FROM THE VIDEO GAME THAT YOU ARE PLAYING?

A .. A thrilling game with lots of action

B .. Competitive play

C .. A test of my fast reactions

D .. To discover a cool new story

E .. The chance to learn something new

2. WHAT ARE THE SKILLS THAT MAKE YOU A GREAT GAMER?

A .. I can make decisions really quickly

B .. I'm a strategic genius

C .. My hand-eye coordination is out of this world

D .. I'm patient and great at thinking my way out of tricky situations

E .. My problem-solving ability

3. WHO DO YOU LIKE TO PLAY GAMES WITH?

A .. Lots of friends, either at my place, or online

B .. With my team mates

C .. I don't care. I'm usually too caught up in the game

D .. Interesting characters that I meet in the game

E .. Anyone who wants to learn and have fun

4. ARE YOU COMPETITIVE WHEN IT COMES TO GAMING?

A .. Totally! I want to be the last one standing

B .. Yes, but I want to win it for my club

C .. Winning is cool, but excitement is more important

D .. We all win when the game has an amazing story

E .. If I don't win, it's no big deal

5. WHAT DO YOU LIKE TO DO WHEN YOU'RE NOT GAMING?

A .. I'm always gaming!

B .. Planning my strategy for the next game

C .. Itching to get going on another game

D .. Thinking about where I'd like to explore next

E .. Something active outdoors

6. HOW LONG DO YOU LIKE AN INDIVIDUAL GAME TO LAST?

A .. I like a game to be quick and intense

B .. It doesn't matter – I play to the whistle

C .. Long enough for me to get the better of my rivals

D .. On and on. I lose sense of time

E .. Until I want to do something else

7. DO YOU DISCUSS YOUR FAVOURITE GAMES WITH YOUR FRIENDS?

A .. Only after I've beaten them

B .. It's a great way of getting new tips

C .. No. I might let slip some of my secret moves

D .. Yes, to relive the experience afterwards

E .. Yes, among other things

8. HOW DO YOU LIKE TO FEEL AFTER YOU'VE FINISHED PLAYING A GAME?

A .. I've had a thrilling time with friends

B .. We've given it our best shot

C .. I've still got the fastest moves in town

D .. I've explored new places and met interesting characters

E .. I've got new knowledge or skills

ANSWERS

MOSTLY As It's all about the action for you, preferably in a game with lots of others playing. Multiplayer online games and action-adventure titles will give you the chance to make lots of decisions, compete against others, and enjoy the thrills. *See page 32 & 36*

MOSTLY Bs You're sporty and competitive with bags of energy. Put that to good use with sports games that allow you to make the best use of your tactical knowledge, or try some activity games where you can jump around and let loose. *See page 44 & 50*

MOSTLY Cs You're quick on the trigger, or the handset, with great reactions that make you a fiend to beat in combat and driving games. It's almost as if you don't have to think about what you're doing. *See page 42 & 46*

MOSTLY Ds Gaming is a pleasure to be enjoyed patiently for you. Strategy or fantasy games allow you to take a journey with your favourite characters, exploring new worlds and becoming immersed in them. *See page 38 & 48*

MOSTLY Es You like games, but it's just one of your things. With your thirst for knowledge, educational games let you test yourself, while simulations put you in control of the situation. *See page 34 & 40*

CREATE
YOUR
GAMER
PROFILE

Your gamer profile is your introduction to other players. It gives you an identity, tells others a bit about you, and helps them to remember you.

You probably want to start gaming as soon as possible, but it's worth giving your profile a bit of thought. Once completed, it may cost money to make changes to things like your gamer name.

Don't just choose the first things that you think are funny or cool. Within a few days, you might decide they are silly or rude. It's also important to make sure that your profile doesn't include information that might identify you.

NAME:

NICKNAME:

AGE:

MOTTO:

YOUR SKILLS:

YOUR STRENGTHS:

_____

_____

_____

_____

_____

YOUR WEAKNESSES:

_____

_____

_____

_____

_____

_____

YOUR FRIENDS:

_____

_____

_____

_____

_____

YOUR RECORDS:

_____

_____

_____

_____

_____

DESIGN YOUR OWN AVATAR

DRAW YOUR AVATAR HERE

Avatars are a fun way to show your gaming personality to other players. You can create your own unique character using the brilliant tools available on consoles and websites. You can go into amazing detail, changing how your avatar looks, what it wears and even its facial expression.

MULTIPLAYER ONLINE

These games allow large numbers of players to take part in the same game at the same time. You can be one of hundreds of characters taking part in the action.

Sometimes called massively multiplayer online games, or MMOGs, these games are played on the internet so you can end up playing other gamers from anywhere in the world. MMOGs usually take place in a world where players compete or work together to achieve something, such as building a world, going on a journey, or fighting each other to be the champion.

You can even chat to other players and send them messages to get them onside.

Players have to download software to their computer or playing device in order to play MMOGs. These games are often free to play the basic version, but players can buy stuff* to make their characters look better, to help them compete, or to get to another level.

* Always ask an adult for permission before spending money on games.

✪✪✪✪✪ GAMES ✪✪✪✪✪

MINECRAFT

If you like building things, Minecraft is a great game to create a world, a building, or anything you can think of. You can link with friends to create and explore, or join larger groups in specially created virtual worlds.

FORTNITE

Players compete to be the last one standing in shooter game Fortnite. Each game only lasts about twenty minutes, if you make it to the end. You can play it solo or team up in the multiplayer version.

ROBLOX

With Roblox, you can create your own games, or play fun games that have been made by other Roblox users. As well as the usual combat or driving games, you can manage a fast food restaurant, be a catwalk model, or survive a storm.

✪ SIMULATION ✪

Simulation games, or 'sims', aim to get as close to putting you in a real life situation as is possible in a game. You are in charge of the controls to determine what happens next.

Vehicle simulation games are among the most popular as they let you get into the driving seat of a vehicle that you're too young to drive, like a car, or something that you may never control, like a jet fighter, train, or even a bus. The games designers try and copy the experience of controlling these vehicles to make it as close to the real thing as you can imagine, so you can land a plane at a real life airport, or drive a racing car around a Formula 1 circuit.

Sim games also let you build a city, run a business or look after animals. There is no right or wrong way to play the games, so you learn by trial and error.

✪✪✪✪✪ GAMES ✪✪✪✪✪

GRAN TURISMO

Choose from more than 100 racing cars and then race around various tracks. The latest versions of the game have online play so you can race to become a driving champion.

THE SIMS

You manage the lives of virtual people called Sims, helping them work, play and interact with other Sims. Some people love creating the perfect house for their Sims, while others are more interested in their story. It's up to you.

ZOO TYCOON

Control your own animal kingdom. As well as buying animals and taking care of them, you are in charge of making sure that the zoo is a successful business that lots of people want to visit.

ACTION AND ADVENTURE

As the name suggests, action-adventure games mix the action that makes a game exciting, with an element of adventure that keeps your interest for longer. It's like two games in one.

Purely action games are all about reactions and skills and are usually quite fast and exciting. With action-adventure, you get this along with the problem solving that comes with an adventure game where you might go on a journey.

Action-adventure covers a really broad range of games and some will have more action than adventure elements, or the other way around. There is usually a storyline, lots of characters, and dialogue between the characters as you look to solve puzzles to continue your character's journey through various levels.

Hand-eye coordination and great player skills are also important as you have to outwit your opponents, or bash them up!

✪✪✪✪✪ GAMES ✪✪✪✪✪

HOW TO TRAIN YOUR DRAGON

You train to become a Viking dragon trainer, creating your dragon and improving its speed, power and fire. As well as battling other dragons, you can explore the island of Berk, which is their home.

THE LEGEND OF ZELDA

Help guide the game's hero, Link, through the realm of Hyrule, fighting monsters and solving puzzles. There are lots of areas to explore and you'll need to develop survival skills such as hunting and cooking.

LEGO HARRY POTTER

Collect, explore and solve puzzles with Harry and his Hogwarts chums as they go through their wizard training. Casting spells, making potions and collecting bricks are all part of the fun and help to unlock bonus levels in the game.

✪✪✪ STRATEGY ✪✪✪

Not all games are quick to play and over in a flash. Strategy games are all about thinking carefully about what you want to achieve and how you are going to do it.

In strategy games you have to make decisions all the time, and each decision you make will have an effect on what happens next. Because of this, every time you play the game should be different. It also means that games take a long time to play – sometimes days or even weeks. That doesn't matter though, because the games are so interesting and you become absorbed in the fantasy worlds.

Some strategy games might seem tough to play as they are generally aimed at older gamers, but if you stick with them, you will be rewarded. They're also a good way of involving friends who can give you advice.

✪✪✪✪✪ GAMES ✪✪✪✪✪

CHESS

Chess is the original strategy game, based on ancient war strategy. As well as playing on a board, there are lots of video game versions that allow you to play against friends, the computer, or players from around the world.

MARIO + RABBIDS

Mario and his friends have to try and solve the chaos that Rabbids bring to Mushroom Kingdom when they misuse a new energy invention. You go through different worlds and levels, solving problems, having battles and helping Mario.

80 DAYS

Based on Jules Verne's book *Around the World in 80 Days*, this game puts you in charge of Phileas Fogg's travel arrangements. Make sure he makes the right decisions and ensure that Fogg doesn't miss his connections as he explores the Earth.

✪✪ EDUCATIONAL ✪✪

Video games can be educational, helping you with school learning as well as improving concentration, observation, and problem-solving ability. You just need to know which games to choose to boost your brain power.

Research has shown that rather than being a waste of time, as some adults claim, video games help in many areas. Some games are tailored towards learning a particular skill, such as typing.

Other advantages of playing games are that they help with hand to eye coordination and are even a way of improving social relation skills, meaning that you are better at making friends and communicating with people.

Certain games teach very specific things, such as helping you become better at maths or English, learning a foreign language, or even conducting science experiments ... without the risk of blowing the house up!

✪✪✪✪✪ GAMES ✪✪✪✪✪

MENSA ACADEMY

Train your brain through a series of questions and challenges that cover the five areas of numeracy, language, logic, memory, and visual. It has more than 100 replayable levels.

JUNIOR BRAIN TRAINER

This collection of games encourages you to spend a bit of time each day playing games that can help with reading, writing, spelling, problem solving and more. Completing tasks unlocks games as a reward.

MATH BLASTER

Join Blaster Academy and go through training missions to learn how to protect the universe. The missions are all maths games that involve solving equations to win.

✪✪✪✪ COMBAT ✪✪✪✪

Everyone loves a trial of strength, and in the gaming world nobody really gets hurt, which is good. Choose your weapons, tool up and practise to become the fiercest warrior.

Combat games come in a variety of forms, but usually involve learning to combine defensive blocks with attack moves, and putting together 'combos' of moves to outfox your opponent. There are sometimes secret moves that you can discover as you play the game more.

Some games are one-on-one, while others can have multiple fighters at once. Choosing the right weapons or warrior is important as each of them will have their own strengths and weaknesses, and you may find that you are better with some weapons than others.

It is important to remember that in fight games it's all pretend. Keep it on screen and don't try it at home.

✪✪✪✪✪ GAMES ✪✪✪✪✪

FORTNITE

Use your fighting skills and cooperation to try and survive being beaten by other players. Games are action-packed and  can be over very quickly, if you're caught out. Although the basic game is free, you can buy V-Bucks* to buy tools, weapons, outfits and other items.

SPLATOON

Characters called Inklings squirt coloured ink at their opponents to take over their space or splat them. Players can take part in colourful contests on their own or in teams of up to four.

LEGO MARVEL SUPER HEROES

You can choose from many of your favourite Marvel characters, including the Avengers, the Fantastic Four, and X-Men. You can then use their super skills to fight, explore and solve puzzles.

* Always ask an adult for permission before spending money on games.

✪✪✪✪✪ SPORT ✪✪✪✪✪

You don't have to be super sporty to enjoy sports video games. The skills you need are different from those required for the real thing, but that doesn't mean they are any less fun.

Every game has its own rules and tactics, and these days, every game seems to have its own video game version. Some, like football, are well known and have been around for a long time. Others are newer and may be less familiar, but they can be just as challenging. You can try golf, skateboarding, cycling, ice hockey, rugby and more, all from your own home.

Sports games are becoming more and more like the real thing. The visuals are getting better all the time, and players have more control. You can even customise sport kits and celebrations in some games.

✪✪✪✪✪ GAMES ✪✪✪✪✪

MARIO TENNIS

Despite his lack of height, Mario can get around the tennis court like a pro. This game has him playing against some of the classic Mario characters, including Luigi, Donkey Kong, Peach and Bowser.

FIFA

Football is the world's number one game, and FIFA is the top video game. Every year the latest version lets fans take control of the best teams and players in the world.

INFINITE MINI GOLF

Everyone loves crazy golf, and this game lets you play the craziest courses around, as well as designing your own holes. With thousands of holes created by players, there's always a new challenge.

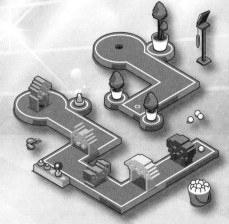

✪✪✪✪ DRIVING ✪✪✪✪

**There are lots of driving games to choose from,
depending on what type of vehicles you like.
The driving experience can be real or imaginary.**

Part of the fun of any driving game is choosing what kind of vehicle you
want to drive, and games have a huge choice. You can also customise
things like car colour, types of wheels and your driving outfit.

The action in some driving games takes place on race tracks that are
designed to look just like the ones that real life drivers compete on.
Others have a more fantasy feel to them and you may have to avoid
some pretty odd obstacles, and drive through strange course designs.
Whatever the type of game, the driver has to combine speed and skill
and the faster you go, the harder it can be
to stay completely on track.

✪✪✪✪✪ GAMES ✪✪✪✪✪

MARIO KART

Mario and his friends race round a series of amazing courses collecting power-ups that help them to gain speed on their rivals. Different modes let you race in different ways such as times trials or in battle mode.

GRAN TURISMO

Some people think this is one of the best video games ever. You can play it in arcade mode, which lets you choose your car and the track, or sim mode, where you race to win driver licences which allow you to enter more challenging races.

ROCKET LEAGUE

Is it a driving game, or is it a football game? It's both! You use your driving skills to score goals against an opposing team as you try and drive up the league.

CARS

Based on the film series, *Cars* has you driving Lightning McQueen to win races, collect weapons and power-ups, and practise stunts.

✪✪✪✪ FANTASY ✪✪✪✪

These games can take place in amazing worlds that are limited only by the imagination of the people who made the game and the players. They can take you anywhere – back in history, into space, or into imagined worlds.

Fantasy games are more about going on a journey and experiencing a story, rather than all out action. However, there can be action too, keeping things interesting.

Players usually take on the identity of a character and make decisions for them. This is called role playing – they're sometimes called RPGs, or role playing games – and lets you shape the character's storyline.

The plot in fantasy games develops gradually so you can play the games over a long period of time with friends who have their own characters. You can cooperate with other characters or challenge them as you go on your journey.

✪✪✪✪✪ GAMES ✪✪✪✪✪

POKÉMON

While trying to catch all of the Pokémon, you take control of the Pokémon trainer directing them through a fantasy world.

MOSS

In this action fantasy game, players guide a little mouse character, Quill, through a fairy tale, as it looks to save the world from danger. Quill needs to solve problems, overcome obstacles and take part in sword fights as the journey progresses.

THE LEGEND OF ZELDA

The main character, Link, travels through the kingdom of Hyrule after waking up from a long sleep. Players help him relearn about his kingdom, fighting monsters, problem solving and exploring as he goes.

✪✪✪ ACTIVITY ✪✪✪

When you have energy to burn, activity-based games give you an excuse to get off the sofa and jump around, swing your arms, or shout the house down.

There are a number of activity games that use your body movements to play the game. Sensors from the console can pick up what you are doing and transfer them to a character in the game.

Some of these games need extra pieces of equipment, such as special handsets, floormats, musical instruments, or microphones. Although these mean you have to spend some more money, they make the games more interactive and fun to play.

These activity games are a mix of games that let you do something that you enjoy, with a competitive element that lets you gain points and try to beat family and friends.

☆☆☆☆☆ GAMES ☆☆☆☆☆

JUST DANCE

Dancers have to copy moves shown on screen, collecting points for accuracy and earning bonus points for gold moves. Each game comes with a collection of great pop songs to bust moves to all evening.

SINGSTAR

If you're more of a singer than a dancer, SingStar lets you sing along to your favourite hits, but you have to be able to sing in time and in tune to get the best score.

WII SPORTS

This was one of the first games to use a motion-sensing controller that allows you to hit a tennis ball or baseball, bowl, play golf or box. Just be careful you don't get too excited and knock someone over.

GUITAR HERO

Rock out to the biggest and best bands using a guitar-shaped control that you wear around your neck. Four coloured buttons are used to follow the track that is playing on screen. It sounds easy, but it's not.

LEVEL
UP

GAMIFY YOUR DAY

They say that life is just a game, and it can be if you award yourself points for doing good stuff. Each deed scores points that could add up to treats, or even some extra gaming time if your parents agree.

Wake up on time
+10

Start the day as you mean to go on by staying on schedule.

Stay hydrated
+10

Make sure you drink plenty of water. It's healthier than sugary drinks.

Take out the rubbish
+25

Bin duty scores big points especially if you recycle as well.

Eat a healthy breakfast
+15

It's the most important meal of the day and fuel for your body and brain.

REWARD

You got over 50 points! Give yourself a treat for all your great work.

Pay someone a compliment
+15

It is so important to make people feel acknowledged and loved.

Phone your relatives

+15

It's good to talk to someone who hasn't heard from you in a while.

REWARD

You got 100 points! You win 15 minutes of extra screen time.

Make a cup of tea

+10

Adults love tea. Just be careful with the hot water.

Brush your teeth

+15

– until they're gleaming. And don't forget to floss.

Tidy your room

+10

Probably a good idea to do this on bin night. Don't forget under the bed.

Eat your 5-a-day

+30

Fruit and vegetables are good for you and can make you more alert.

Charge batteries

+20

So that they're ready when you're allowed to start gaming again.

WINNER

SNACK ATTACKS

Even the most obsessed gamer needs to grab a bite, but what is the best way to fuel a games marathon?

SANDWICHES

The original finger food was invented so that the 4th Earl of Sandwich could keep gaming – what better recommendation do you need? The choice of fillings will keep even the fussiest eater happy. Your gamer buddies can easily attack a stack of sandwiches between levels.

HUMMUS AND VEGGIES

Dips are a great way to cram in some tasty calories, and hummus, which is made from chickpeas, provides plenty of carbohydrates to keep you going. Chopped fresh vegetables, such as pepper, carrot sticks, cucumber and celery are best for scooping up the delicious dip.

SMOOTHIES

It's important to remember to drink while playing, so load up on glasses of water. You can also blend some of your favourite fruit into smoothies. As well as providing vitamins and minerals to keep your performance up, superfoods like blueberries can even improve your concentration.

NUTS AND DRIED FRUIT

When you only have one hand free, it's useful to have some scoopable eats to hand. The sweet and savoury combination of nuts and dried fruit is incredibly moreish and better for you than a handful of cookies (honest).

SUSHI

These tasty rice rolls are fairly easy to get hold of, or you can even try making your own. (Yeah, right!) The sticky rice provides plenty of carbohydrates to keep you going,

while the fillings of fish – a brain food – or vegetables keep things healthy.

CHOCOLATE

Every games session is allowed one 'naughty' food, but go easy on the sweeties. Even better, have a small piece of dark chocolate. It can take some getting used to but scientists think that dark chocolate can boost your memory by improving blood flow to the brain. Think about that!

ALLERGY WARNING

Always check before you offer anything to your friends. If you are unsure, always check with a responsible adult.

WHAT TO DO IF YOU'RE BEING BULLIED ONLINE

Bullying online, or cyberbullying, is communication from someone else that makes you feel sad or uncomfortable, and that you want to stop.

It is just as important to tackle it as any other type of bullying, and there are things that you can do.

A good starting point is telling someone you trust what is going on. You don't have to deal with bullying alone.

WHAT TO DO IF YOU'RE BEING BULLIED

- Don't keep it to yourself or try to deal with it alone.
- It helps to talk, so tell an adult you trust. If it's serious, tell the police. The person may be bullying others too.
- Don't reply to any nasty messages you receive. Keep the messages that you've been sent so you can show someone.
- Don't share, comment, or like any bullying posts. Sharing or commenting could make the bullying worse. It can be tackled, so don't be dispirited.

WHAT TO DO IF YOU THINK YOU'RE BULLYING SOMEONE

- The first step is realizing that your behaviour could be affecting others. If someone is upset and has asked you to stop doing something, it's a sign.
- Understand that we all make mistakes and it doesn't make you a bad person.
- Tell someone you trust, like a parent or teacher. They may be able to offer advice about what to do.
- Go back and delete any upsetting comments you've written.
- Talk to others involved and encourage them to stop the bullying.
- Apologize to the person who was bullied and offer them support.
- Learn from what has happened and change the way you act in the future.

NEXT
LEVEL

LOADING IDEA ...

DESIGN YOUR OWN GAME

After playing a whole batch of games, you may start to get some ideas of your own. There's always room for another game in the world, so why shouldn't it be one that you have designed?

Once you have come up with the basic idea for your game, you can start to plan it out with these special design pages. They will take you through the important stages you need to take an idea and make it into something that you can actually play.

Start at the beginning and work your way through each of the stages. Put in as much detail as you can.

CONCEPT

1. What is the name of the game?

_____

2. What type of game is it? (tick box)

☐   Multiplayer online game   ☐   Combat game

☐   Simulation game   ☐   Sport game

☐   Action-adventure game   ☐   Driving game

☐   Strategy game   ☐   Fantasy game

☐   Educational game   ☐   Activity game

3. Is it single player or multiplayer?

☐   Single player   ☐   Multiplayer

4. How difficult is the game?

_____

5. How long will it take the average player to complete?

_____

DESCRIBE THE GAME PLOT.

(What do you have to do? How do you win?)

_____

_____

_____

_____

_____

_____

_____

_____

_____

_____

WHO ARE THE GAME'S CHARACTERS?

(What are their names and what do they look like? You can draw them here.)

DRAW THE GAME LANDSCAPE.

(Where does it take part? Draw it here. Maybe you could create a map.)

CONGRATULATIONS!

You're on your way to designing your first game.

GAME
ON

GAMER

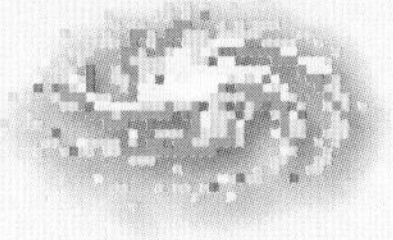

LOG

_____

_____

_____

_____

_____

_____

_____

_____

_____

_____

GAMER

LOG

GAMER

LOG

GLOSSARY

Anonymity – this means that other gamers don't know your real identity or details such as your age or where you live. Anonymity is important to keep yourself safe online.

Avatar – the character that represents you in a game. These can be customised and personalised so that each avatar is as individual as you are.

Cartridge – back in the old days, games didn't come on discs or online. They were loaded into the console as large plastic cartridges. Some handheld consoles still have cartridge systems, but they are much smaller.

Console – the unit that you use to play games through, such as PlayStation, Xbox, Wii, and Nintendo Switch. Some games can only be played on certain consoles, so make sure that the console you choose has the games you like.

Customisation – games let you choose certain elements for your game character so that it is different from those of other people. This may include choosing the type of character for the game, their clothes, weapons, tools or vehicles. Customising your character can be as much fun as playing the game.

Cyberbullying – this is bullying online. If someone says or does anything to you during a game, or online, that makes you feel sad or uncomfortable, then it is bullying. Don't keep it to yourself. Tell a responsible adult or someone you trust.

Game name – the name you use when you are playing. Be as inventive as you like. Ninjastrike2000 is a bit more interesting than Jack1.

Operating system – the software that controls your console, tablet or computer. This changes all the time and newer games will sometimes only work with devices that have newer operating systems.

Personal information – anything that can help identify you as an individual, such as your name, email, passwords, birthday, school, or address. It is important to keep your personal information safe and private.

Simulation – games that recreate real world situations and put you in charge. That can mean anything from controlling the lives of characters in an imaginary world, to trying to land a jumbo jet.

Spyware – software that is secretly added to your computer to spy on you or steal your details. Make sure that you have the most up to date software to protect you against this.

V-Bucks – a cybercurrency, or digital money, that can be used to buy stuff in the game Fortnite. Other games have their own cybercurrencies that let you buy tools and weapons, or access new parts of a game. Remember that these currencies cost real money so always ask an adult before you buy.

Virus – software that can get on to your device and stop it working properly. Be careful about opening emails or clicking on links from people you don't know. They could result in a virus.